Published by Jaico Publishing House
A-2 Jash Chambers, 7-A Sir Phirozshah Mehta Road
Fort, Mumbai - 400 001
jaicopub@jaicobooks.com
www.jaicobooks.com

Published in arrangement with
The Creative Company
123 South Broad Street
Mankato, MN 56001
USA

Design and production by The Design Lab
Art direction by Rita Marshall

Photographs by Alamy (Ann and Steve Toon), Getty Images (Panoramic Images, Tim Laman, Michael Poliza, Christopher Scott, Art Wolfe), and iStockphoto (Steven Allan, John Carnemolla, Chris Fourie, Nikita Golovanov, Robert Hardholt, Peter Malsbury)

ELEPHANTS
ISBN 978-81-8495-339-8

First Jaico Impression: 2012

Printed by
Aegean Offset Printers
220 B, Udyog Kendra – 1,
Greater Noida, UP - 201306, India

AMAZING ANIMALS

ELEPHANTS

KATE RIGGS

JAICO PUBLISHING HOUSE
Ahmedabad Bangalore Bhopal Bhubaneswar Chennai
Delhi Hyderabad Kolkata Lucknow Mumbai

A full-grown elephant can be more than 13 feet (4 m) tall

Elephants are the largest land animals in the world. There are three kinds of elephants living today. Wild elephants live on the **continents** of Africa and Asia.

continents Earth's seven big pieces of land

Elephants have special noses called trunks. Long teeth called tusks stick out on both sides of the trunk. Elephants have rough skin and big, floppy ears. An elephant flaps its ears when it is hot.

Elephants flap their ears like fans to help cool off

Male elephants are bigger than females. Male African elephants can weigh up to 18,000 pounds (8,165 kg). Asian elephants weigh about 12,000 pounds (5,440 kg).

A male African elephant can weigh as much as four cars

Asian elephants live where there are many green plants

There are two kinds of African elephants. African bush elephants live on the **savannas**. They are the biggest elephants. African forest elephants live in jungles. Asian elephants live in wet, grassy parts of southern Asia.

savannas flat, hot lands covered with grass and a few trees

Elephants need to eat about 220 pounds (100 kg) of food a day

Elephants are plant eaters. They use their trunks to grab leaves off trees. They eat grass off the ground. And they eat seeds and fruits off other plants. Sometimes elephants even eat **crops**.

crops plants people grow for food

Mothers and calves may "hold hands" with their trunks

A mother elephant has one **calf** at a time. A calf is three feet (0.9 m) tall when it is born. Calves stay close to their mothers until they are four or five years old. Older elephants help keep calves safe from **predators** such as lions and hyenas. Wild elephants can live 60 to 80 years.

calf a baby elephant

predators animals that kill and eat other animals

Elephants live in family groups called herds. Most herds have about 6 to 12 elephants. The leaders of a herd are the oldest female elephants. Elephants spend a lot of time walking around to find food.

An elephant herd may travel a long way to find food

Mud cools elephants on hot days and keeps bugs away

Elephants nap a lot. They spend time drinking and bathing, too. They use their trunks to drink and spray water. Elephants play in the water and mud when it is very hot.

Today, some people go to Africa or Asia to see elephants in the wild. Other people visit zoos to see elephants. It is fun to see these big animals flap their ears and shake their trunks!

A big elephant's trunk can weigh 300 pounds (136 kg).

An Elephant Story

Why is an elephant's trunk so long? A man named Rudyard (*RUD-yerd*) Kipling wrote a story about this. A curious young elephant once asked a crocodile what he ate for dinner. The crocodile told the elephant to lean in close so he could tell him. Then the crocodile grabbed onto the young elephant's nose and tried to eat him! The crocodile pulled and pulled until the trunk grew as long as it is today!

Read More

Gibbons, Gail. *Elephants of Africa.* New York: Holiday House, 2008.

Magloff, Lisa. *Elephant.* New York: DK Publishing, 2005.

Web Sites

Enchanted Learning: Elephants
http://www.enchantedlearning.com/subjects/mammals/elephant/Elephantcoloring.shtml
This site has elephant facts and a picture to color.

National Geographic Kids Creature Feature: African Elephants
http://kids.nationalgeographic.com/Animals/CreatureFeature/African-elephant
This site has pictures and videos of African elephants.

Index